Walking With You for

Published by:
Sufficient Grace Ministries for Women, Inc.
P.O. Box 243
Deshler, Ohio 43516

This book is a combination of writings from Kelly Gerken and a compilation of stories from grieving fathers around the world.

Edited and formatted by: Emily Jetter

Cover Image: Bethany Conkel

Cover Design: Bethany Conkel, Maria Elkins

ISBN-13: 978-1720518136

ISBN-10: 1720518130

Special thanks to the SGM team and the brave and strong fathers who have contributed thoughts from the most sacred places of their hearts. It is our privilege to walk this path with so many amazing parents. We remember each of your precious children with you. Thank you for offering the wisdom you have gleaned, in hopes that other mothers and fathers will know they do not walk alone.

Rejoice with those who rejoice,

and weep with those who weep.

~ Romans 12:15

TABLE OF CONTENTS

Introduction

Years ago, a nurse asked me if Sufficient Grace Ministries offered any resources specifically for fathers. I wasn't sure if grieving fathers would want a lot of resources, if they would want to talk in the moments of raw grief. My husband was quiet and withdrawn. He didn't seem to want a lot of attention when we lost our twin daughters born still at 26 weeks and later our newborn son. I was surprised to learn just how wrong I was, as we delved further into serving bereaved parents, expanding our services to include in-person support as comfort doulas and remembrance photographers. I have watched husbands at the bedside of their partners, kissing tiny babies goodbye, desperate to find something to fix all the broken in that moment. And, I've read the words of fathers, while working on this book for dads. It has been our privilege to read the powerful words from the brave men who contributed to this project.

And, what I learned from these amazing fathers comforted my own aching mother/wife heart. You see, sometimes in the quiet, the doubt creeps in for mothers (wives/partners), and the fact that we grieve differently leaves us feeling alone. The helplessness makes him pull away...because he's at a loss as to how to make this broken right. He can't fix it...so he hides. Or works a lot. Or escapes any way he can. When that happens, because of the words from the brave fathers in this book, I tell those hurting moms: *"He loves you. He loves you and he loves your baby. In the midst of all the broken...remember that. Don't think he doesn't care about you...or your child. He does...so much. It just undoes a man not to be able to protect those he loves the most...not to be able to make the wrongs right or dry his wife's tears. It isn't because he doesn't care. It's because he does."*

4

It is our prayer that the words in this booklet, spoken by fathers to fathers will encourage you in the moments when you feel overwhelmed by the broken things you can't fix, and the missing of your baby, or the pain of your wife, or the truth that everything is changed.

Please know that you are not alone.

If You Have Just Received a Diagnosis Or Are Currently At The Hospital

Matt -
Take pictures of your child. They are painful at the moment; they are awful to have to go through. But a year later, I am very happy that we took them. It is one of the few things we have to remember him by. Also, hold them. It is painful, agonizing, and heart wrenching. But it is your only chance. You don't get to bring your baby home, so hold them while you can. I also feel that men grieve later for their child. Women go through so many changes in their body, and they are ripped from motherhood so fast. For a father, we focus on helping the mother grieve, to support her, and in our situation, to help take care of the children we had before while my wife recovered from her C-section. So at the time of losing our son, I didn't have the opportunity or the ability to grieve. I had to be that rock for my family. Later, after we got back into our routines, I noticed that I had a lot more triggers than before, and memories and reminders of what happened hit me harder.

Jacob -
Having those memories of my son has helped. Having the book with his footprints allowed me to design a tattoo that I look at daily.

Justin -
I wish I had been warned about how discombobulated I would feel after the initial shock wore off. I struggled to know my place in all of the chaos that was taking place around me. I went along with things more than I would normally and I didn't ask enough questions. Hold your baby. Hold him for as long as you like. Hold him as though he were alive. You will not get another chance.

Depending on the age of your baby at the time of loss and hospital policy, you will have forms to fill out. You will likely face decisions you never thought you'd be considering. If there's time, it would be good to discuss some of the possibilities with your partner. This will alleviate leaving one person responsible for making these difficult decisions. It's important to understand and communicate your feelings to one another, even in the midst of this very painful time.

- If possible, would you like to see or hold your baby?
- What kind of mementos are available to honor your baby's life?
- Will there be time to make tangible memories? Take pictures?
- What options are available as a final resting place for your baby's remains?
  1. Allow the hospital to keep baby
  2. Cremation
  3. Take baby home for burial
  4. Funeral arrangements/Cemetery
  5. Some hospitals have memorial gardens

What is comforting to you as a father may be different than what is comforting to your wife. It is important to understand and respect the needs of your partner, even as you express your own needs. Many fathers feel protective and may feel concern about participating in memory-making or taking pictures. No one considers what they may wish to do if their baby dies. That isn't something we contemplate as a society, until we are faced with the painful reality. At first, it may seem strange to take pictures or spend time creating tangible memories with your baby. But, most parents are grateful, as time passes, that they spent the time holding their baby and celebrating the life of their precious little one. Even if you feel uncomfortable with this, please allow your wife/partner to take the time to get pictures and make memories if she wishes. This is very important for her healing. It may also be helpful for your heart in time as well, even if you feel uncomfortable with it in the moment. This is still your baby. And, all babies are worthy of celebration.

Colleen's father, Larry (who was originally hesitant to get the photographs), powerfully said, *"I like to relive the moments in the pictures, because the pictures tell the story. Her story. I love to see the people in the background, the people who were there with us."*

As a certified perinatal loss support professional (comfort doula), I have worked with many mothers and fathers over the years, supporting families at the hospital and beyond. So many fathers have mentioned that they felt unsure about allowing support staff and remembrance photographers to come alongside them at first. Every one of them expressed later that they were so glad that they decided to allow us to walk with them as a gentle guide in those initial moments creating memories with their babies. Proper support should be parent-centered, not taking away from parents bonding with their baby, but creating an opportunity for parents to spend the time they are given the way that they wish.

No one is more equipped to parent a baby, whether alive or not, than his or her parents.

Even if a baby's life has been brief, there are ways to honor your child's memory.

- A special blanket
- Teddy bear to hold
- An ultrasound picture
- A special song that makes you think of your little one
- Journal your thoughts, dreams, and feelings.
- Write your own letters to your baby
- Taking photos, even of tiny babies is an option
- Praying together
- Naming your baby
- Spend time saying hello and goodbye. Do anything special to you that you're able to do with your child.
- Special jewelry or other items that you would like with you and baby in a photograph
- A book to read to your baby if you wish
- Music that's special to you
- A special memory book
- Take time to bathe and dress your baby if you choose.
- Keep your child with you as long as you like. Take your time.
- Keep a lock of hair, if possible.
- Baptism/Dedication/Naming Ceremony or other ceremonies that are important to you and your family
- Arrangements should be made to have professional photographers available. There are organizations, such as *Sufficient Grace Ministries*, *Now I Lay Me Down to Sleep* and others who provide photography services for families facing the loss of a baby, free of charge. Other organizations (also *Sufficient Grace Ministries)* offering perinatal hospice services may also offer photography as part of an array of services and support.
- Do not allow others to determine how you spend that time. This is your opportunity to fill a lifetime of memories into moments. Spend it the way you see fit. And, don't rush or allow others to rush you.

Receiving a Life-Limiting Diagnosis

The shock and devastation of hearing that your baby has a life-limiting diagnosis, when you were expecting a joyous outcome, the gift of new life, can shake a parent to the core. Parents are left with many questions, and are often faced with difficult and impossible decisions.

What will it be like to continue a pregnancy, knowing my baby's life will be brief?

What does this mean for our family?

How does such a decision mesh with our faith, our beliefs?

Is organ or tissue donation a possibility for my child?

Will we still get to see our child and form memories with our child?

Doctors offer options a parent never thought they would face:
- Perinatal Hospice (Comfort Care) – Defined below
- Palliative Care with some medical intervention (if possible)
- Compassionate Induction – delivering a baby early at the hospital, usually by medically inducing labor. Baby typically passes shortly after birth.
- Termination

Perinatal hospice offers another way to look at a life-limiting diagnosis in the womb. It gives parents the option to continue their pregnancy, cherishing whatever time they are given with their baby. It is referred to as "hospice in the womb," which includes birth planning and support after baby's birth until the baby's death, and beyond.

Hope replaces some of the hopelessness, as parents are empowered to make decisions on behalf of their baby and family. It doesn't take away the agony of the impending loss, but there is a sweet gift in giving your baby and yourself, the opportunity to embrace his life, no matter how brief. For more information, resources, support, or help creating a birth plan, visit: sufficientgraceministries.org

The Number One Thing
We Hear From Grieving Fathers

Men and women grieve differently, and the focus is often on the mother. The struggles fathers face after the loss of a baby are twofold. A father is not only grieving the loss of his baby, but often the added struggle he feels for the grief of his partner. A husband wants to protect his wife and family, to make it better. This is a hurt he could not protect her from, pain he cannot make better. Our hearts go out to the unique position a father is left in as he navigates through this grief, often quietly and with little support.

The number one thing we heard from the fathers interviewed for this book was their immense concern for their wives/partners.

Dan -
There is no right way or wrong way to grieve. Everyone does it at their own pace and in their own way. However you do it, there are two things to remember. First, your wife. Make sure she is taken care of. I remember taking Nancy to the doctor's office, the morning after the ER and everyone asking me how I was. At that point, I didn't care how I was doing. All I cared about was taking care of Nancy. I would worry about myself later. Second, your faith. Don't lose faith in God. I went through a stage where I was so mad at God for what we were going through. But, I eventually realized that there was a reason for what we were going through.

Anthony -
There were moments when you just want to break down but feel you can't because you have to remain strong. I didn't share my emotions as much and I'm sure they weren't as strong as my wife

but I have had moments when I had hurt and teared up over everything. People may think a father isn't affected as strongly but they are. They just may not show it.

Aaron -

As a husband and father, I would tell you that supporting my wife spiritually, emotionally, and physically as much as possible, and seeing my wife and our surviving twin through the delivery and the following stay in NICU were, of course, my first priorities.

One of the most difficult things I had to deal with was the constant input of co-workers, extended family, etc. that I had known for years would come up to me and ask how my wife was doing. I appreciated their concern and I was also most concerned about how my wife was doing, but the majority of these people never asked how I was doing.

Also, a comment that I heard many times that really hurt was, "Aaron, just remember that this is going to be a lot harder on your wife." At times, I felt that people didn't recognize that this was my child as well.

In my opinion it would be so great if there was a way to educate the public that an infant loss is an emotionally devastating event for Fathers as well as Mothers. I feel that part of my responsibility to my wife is to be her protector. I will always place her needs above my own. It would have meant so much to me to know that there were those who recognized that I was hurting

Jeff -
I think it is important for families dealing with loss to understand that each person deals with grief differently. I have found the mothers are usually affected most; after all, they are the ones with the initial bond of carrying within the womb to diminish the grief experienced by myself or other fathers, I just think it is more powerful within the female.

I was far more concerned with making sure that my wife was dealing with things, prior to being concerned with myself. If my feeling associated with grief was getting the better of me, I would make a date with my wood pile and get some frustrations out. I never really dealt with my feelings for several months, maybe even a year after the loss.

Stacy -
Others can support fathers by emphasizing that it is okay to grieve and be weak. It is 100% natural to want to support the spouse and the rest of the family unit. I felt like I had to be strong (despite the tremendous pain and suffering from the loss) for my wife and stepson along with my siblings and everyone else in my family. I wanted to let them know I was going to be 'okay' even if it was so far from the truth at the time.

Kyle -
Unless a father has been down the road of infant death, he has no idea what to do when his baby dies (or is dying). I was a father who was called to suffer this sorrow from infant death, twice – and both situations were very different.

While my own grief confused me, my chief concern was my wife's emotional health. I felt that if she was taken care of, I could handle my own grief. The trouble was, I didn't know what my wife needed. I didn't know what would be healthy for her to see, do and hear the first time around. I knew better the second time, but it was mostly because of what we failed to do correctly the first time.

Mark -
Like you said, our grief is quiet, and often overlooked, and also partly focused on not just the loss of our child, but on the overwhelming grief of the mother.

Tim -
Just take care of your wife. Make sure she's okay.

Dreaming New Dreams

Though we still dream our dreams of you,
We have traded our old dreams for new.
We wonder about your new life in heaven,
We wonder about you nestled ever safe in the Savior's
embrace,
until you fill our arms once more.
Though we still dream our dreams of you,
We have traded our old dreams for new.

~Kelly Gerken

Stories From the Hearts of Grieving Fathers

Matt -
My wife and I were pregnant with our 3rd child. We were at 34 weeks along when my wife started having he signs of labor. We thought it just might be "practice," so we waited through the night. But as they progressed, we knew we had to go in.

*We went in on the morning of December 14, 2016, expecting to bring home a baby. By 8 am, I had found out that our baby was stillborn. I still remember the moment the doctor came in to tell me. Nothing can prepare you for that moment, nothing can ease that pain. There's a quote that I've seen on a few websites that says, "**You were unsure which pain is worse-the shock of what happened or the ache for what never will.**"*

At first, the pain of grieving the loss of our son, Oliver, was what hurt. Having to bury our son was what hurt next. But as we got further away from the date, you start to think about what you will never have. Those birthdays, the trips, the firsts, everything is gone. And as a dad, you walk that path alone most of the time. A lot of the grief groups and talk is about the mother. And yes, the mother goes through an immense amount of pain, grief, anguish-everything. But they have people who reach out to them, people talk to them. As a father, I am expected to be the strong one, the rock for our family. We have to protect our family. And I accept that role willingly. But after we lost our son, I kept asking myself, "How can I protect my family after this? I couldn't protect my unborn child; how can I protect the rest of my family?"

There is no magic cure, there is no answer or group or quote that makes any of it better. Time dulls the pain, the grief, the gut wrenching reality of what happened. But it still hurts. Every day is one piece of the longest journey of your life-living without your child.

Ryan -

My wife was over 21 weeks into her pregnancy. We had a scheduled visit to her OB for a routine checkup with a much anticipated gender reveal and despite having a healthy baby, we found out the baby had low fluid. We were referred immediately to a Maternal Fetal Medicine specialist. After what seemed to be the longest night of our lives, at the next morning's ultrasound, my wife's blood pressure had skyrocketed to 243/134. The ultrasound monitor showed a perfect child but a lack of fluid in the womb. Unbeknownst to us, she was in heart failure.

We consulted with the doctor and we were told that our son would not survive as the fluids were misplaced and retained throughout my wife's body. We were told that my wife was very ill we would need to deliver our son that day to save my wife's life. We were shocked and after asking a few questions it was clear our son would not survive outside the womb. We were whisked away to the special care section of labor and delivery, and I immediately made some of the hardest phone calls I would ever have to make, to her parents.

I knew at this point that we would not be alone in this journey. I knew this would be the most difficult experience I would ever be involved in. My prayer was simple. I prayed to God to bring us through this, give us what we needed to endure the situation. I felt overcome with peace and strength. I immediately was confident that we would get through this. To wrap my head around all the details would have broken me. I put my faith in God.

When we were told it could take hours, our sweet Reid Michael was born just a little over an hour after the first dose of Pitocin. I was able to baptize him and knew he was being welcomed into the kingdom by so many family members in heaven. I noticed the vapor-like mist streaming down from the ceiling. I believe this was Reid's soul leaving the earth. I was at peace and for a moment I was a proud daddy holding a tiny miracle baby. I was so proud. He was a little me right down to my big man hands.

Time stood still for a few short moments when I brought him to meet his mama. She was so sick we had to prop our little man up on some pillows so she could hold him and kiss him, her arms too weak to hold his fragile body. There was underlying sorrow, but God gave us a glimpse of his love. Holding your own flesh and blood in your arms is a humbling experience. The feelings of love and pride were overwhelming. They were raw and real and I couldn't temper them back even though I knew there would also be a tremendous sadness in the experience. I wanted the world to meet him, he was created in love and was our world for the short time we had him. The nursing staff was so empathetic and gave us all the time they could with Reid. I didn't want to say goodbye, but in faith I knew we would be together again someday. I told him how much we loved him and kissed him goodbye.

My wife's medical battle continued for 9 more days. Her life hung in the balance for 3 days following the birth of Reid. They drained over 2 liters of fluid off of sack surrounding her heart. By all medical logic, she should have died as the fluid should have smothered all heart function, but her developing HELLP syndrome raised her blood pressure which counteracted this fluid. Our little man helped save his mama's life by allowing the discovery of an underlying autoimmune complicated heart condition we were all unaware of until these days. I am so proud of that.

Justin -
Samuel was our second child. The pregnancy was fairly normal. On Christmas day after opening presents my wife wasn't feeling well and went to lie down. After a brief period of rest, she contacted her OB who suggested we make a trip to the hospital. We thought worst case scenario we were having this baby that day. Our definition of worst case was forever altered when we were told there was no heartbeat.

Anthony -
My girlfriend (Stephanie) and I, had a baby boy who was diagnosed with Limb Body Wall Complex at 18.6wks gestation. Limb Body Wall Complex is a life limiting prognosis, meaning our baby won't live outside the womb... We were devastated, felt defeated. I was crushed. But I knew that I had to hold my composure, because if Stephanie saw me fall apart, she would

18

break. And I didn't know how to pick up the pieces.

Shortly after finding out about our unborn child's future, her doctor changed, wanted us to terminate the pregnancy right then and there. But, I personally didn't want that to happen to my baby, and we agreed to continue. Stephanie also changed doctors because the OB was really detached with what we wanted.

At 30 weeks, Stephanie went to the hospital an hour away for bleeding, they sent us home because the bleeding stopped/slowed and they felt there was no reason to have us stay. Two days later her water broke, but how it happened was kind of funny. We were sitting on the couch with our other child eating lunch, and she felt a gush. She just took off running, and all I heard was "I CAN'T STOP PEEING!" Then it got quiet. A few seconds passed and I heard "OH Crap! My water broke!".

We went to the hospital and had our son the next day... I was screaming on the inside, infuriated, scared, and all I could do was offer comfort to Stephanie. My family showed up, to offer support, and Kelly (Sufficient Grace Ministries support team) didn't leave us until she felt it was time. She helped set up the Cuddle Cot, even took more photos of our son, who we named Oaken on my camo jacket... Kelly, Naomi, and Kerren's compassion is something I can't forget, and will hold in my heart forever. Because they gave us something that every parent wants... Memories, and more time.

Josh -
Our triplets, Adaryn, Tristan and Clare were born on January 25th, 2015. Adaryn was small but perfect but her siblings, Tristan and Clare were born sleeping.

William -
Lost Kya Ministeri at 20 weeks. My wife was carrying as a surrogate for my sister. We enjoyed her life of about 45 minutes.

Zack -
Our baby was unexpected but extremely loved. The most special

part was just the excitement of learning I was going to be dad to another baby. My wife and I were happier than ever, however sadly our happiness ended when we found out our baby had stopped growing and was well behind in development, as well as having no heartbeat. Although I've experienced this pain three separate times in my life, the pain never becomes less, and having known that pain I never wanted my wife to experience that pain.

Jacob -
Gabriel was our second pregnancy, but the first that had gone past the 1st trimester. Everything seemed to go fine until about 20/21 weeks in. My wife went into labor and there was nothing that they could do to stop it. He was born and survived for a little over 2 hrs.

Scott -
We have lost two very early babies after frozen transfers (IVF).

Jamie -
We lost our son at 18 weeks, and found out at as our midwife couldn't find the heartbeat, and we were sent to a hospital for an ultrasound, who confirmed we had lost our baby.

Brian -
My son, William Arnold Sharp, was stillborn on June 15, 2016 at 35 weeks and 5 days. There was no clinical diagnosis as to the cause of his death; but rather a collection of probabilities. William has an older brother, Benjamin, who was almost four at the time.

One of the most treasured things that I have is a video of my wife and I reading books to William. They were the same books we read to Benjamin when he was little. I have only watched it on his birthday, but just knowing that I can see and hear my wife being a mother to her son warms my soul.

Grieving Together in Marriage/Relationships

One of the biggest issues a couple faces after the initial pain of losing a child, is the struggle in marriage because of lack of communication, stress, or the differences in grieving styles. Many mothers come to us feeling alone in their grief because their husbands grieve quietly. In reading the thoughts of the fathers, it becomes clear that often happens because he is trying to protect her and more concerned with her than in dealing with the pain of his own loss. As difficult as it may be to express these emotions, it will help for your partner to know that she is not alone in her grief, and to share what is on your heart...even if it isn't in the same way that she chooses to express it.

Kyle talks about the importance of something to fight/heal for -
When I saw my wife's grief, it gave me a desire to fight – I wanted her to be happy again. I wouldn't have had that desire if I wouldn't have stopped to notice her pain – or been so wrapped up in my own grief that I didn't acknowledge hers. The harder I worked to help her to heal, the better chance we had of pulling through the grief together.

The result was that we leaned on each other in weak times. Neither of us felt neglected by each other. The result was a stronger marriage.

When we had other children who were grieving, we were strong for them as well. It's amazing what you can conquer when you have love for others and you let it drive you.

Dan -

Nancy and I saw a grief counselor for a little while, but found out that it wasn't for us. We were better talking to each other and with our pastor. There were times when Nancy was doing better and I would regress and vice versa. We have said numerous times that if we didn't have each other to lean on, there would have been no way that we would have been able to be where we are today. It has brought us closer together vs. tearing us apart.

Jeff -

My only concerns initially were making sure my wife was okay, with the things that had to be dealt with, (funeral arrangements, headstone,) We actually kind of rotated our initial ups and downs, when one was up, the other was down and so on. We were able to make sure we were eating properly, and getting enough rest (or as much as was possible). We actually requested people to not make us meals and bring to the house, being there was just the two of us, (we expressed our wishes of privacy to family and friends). For the individuals that insisted on making us food, we requested they wait and make a dish for the gathering after the funeral, (doing it that way certainly decreased the amount of food we would be throwing away).

One day, about a week and a half after our loss, Susan and I were lying in bed talking one morning. I looked at her and said you know, this sucks, we really only have two choices here. Susan said, "What are you talking about?" I said, "We can sit around and feel sorry for ourselves, or we can pick up the remaining pieces and move forward."

Jacob -

If anything it has brought us closer. WE made a vow to each other that we will let the other grieve in whatever manner they desire and support them after. It was agreed that it will NEVER be a taboo subject. So if one needed to talk about it the other would talk it out as well. I cannot put a finger on how much that has helped, but it was one of the key things in our healing process. I don't feel that there is anything my wife did not understand.

Scott -

It's made us stronger. I'm glad that my wife knows that I may not act sad but I do feel bad. I express it and cope with it differently, and that doesn't mean that either of our grieving processes are any more or less valid.

Brian -

*The death of a child forces you to explore and confront emotions that you did not knew existed. I learned that to care for a spouse is exhausting, imperative, and rewarding. Both people need to not only listen in different ways, but talk in different ways. **My wife was a reader of books on grief and the like, however I was a doer/builder of things. We gave each other space and we did not judge the method; we trusted each other.** I was not good at asking for help and she was not good at accepting help; we both thought that inner-strength through an independent grief process was best. When we shed that ridiculous notion we prospered. Now, we have frank conversations about our feelings and it is very empowering to me; I feel that I am listened to, heard, and I feel that she trusts me with her inner-most thoughts. This give me great comfort in the future and our abilities to navigate life together.*

Matt -

It brought us closer. At first it was hard to talk about because it was so raw. But as the days went by, we talked more and more. We talked about how we each felt, what we were struggling with, what we could do to help the other. It made us talk about certain issues we hadn't thought of before. The only thing I wish my wife understood is that sometimes, I wish I didn't have to be that rock. There are days I want to lay in bed and not get up, that there are days where I hardly make it through the day. But it's hard to show that, because we are expected to be strong and solid.

William -

In most ways it has strengthened it. We have become a great team and I think we have proven to each other that we can overcome anything at this point.

Anthony -
The loss of our son hasn't really affected us in a negative way. Even if it tore us apart, we have to stay strong for our living child. I'd like my significant other to know that even though I don't talk about our son, that I haven't forgotten about him, I miss him and I wish he was here too. That I had dreams, hopes and ambitions for him, and they were crushed as well... To not give up and remembering him, say his name as much as you want, he is our son.

Josh -
My wife is more emotionally unavailable and we have different ways of grieving.

Justin -
Ultimately it made our marriage stronger. We learned so much about one another in the process of grief.

Jamie -
That it is just as strong and real as her grief. That my dreams for a family were also lost that day.

Ryan -
Our marriage is stronger by walking this road together. Most of our friends have empathy, but there are no words to substitute for living through the loss of a child. I think something my wife did not understand initially was that I was delaying this process for her. She needed round the clock care weeks after our experience due to her physical health issues following the pregnancy. I wanted to make sure she was able to grieve and I would be able to be there for her during that process. My fear was that if I was grieving myself that I would not be able to help her in the times she needed me.

Stacy -
I didn't realize how much grieving I did not do until my wife left me. It was like the wound was opened all over again in many ways. I have recently started to understand that maybe, maybe my depression grew because of not working through the grief initially. So part of me says my depression made me become unattractive and unmotivated to work at my marriage. As you can see I still felt it was my responsibility to keep the family unit together. Wife is not strong enough to support you in times like this. I would encourage men (now that I can look back) to find another family member or best friend whom they think can take the weight of it all and talk to them on a regular basis on what is hurting and what you are feeling if help groups are not prevalent. Also I found it very helpful to write to my daughter through her virtual memorial website as part of my coping.

Zach -
Surprisingly my wife and I have grown closer in the face of the loss of our baby. It took time for me to best express my feelings with my loss but now my wife better understands my side of the loss.

We asked a few mothers what they wished their partners/spouses understood about their own grief:

Elizabeth -
That I want to be able to freely talk about the pregnancy loss, and for him to understand that need. For him to listen and comfort me when I have bad days.

Paula -
That I WANT to talk about the baby and I want him to bring her up in conversations with me. Often he wouldn't talk about her if I seemed to be having a good moment because he didn't want to remind me and make me sad. Truth is, mamas never forget, not for one second, and we like to talk about our children...even if it brings a tear to our eyes.

Mattie -
I think I would want him to know that I want to know what he needs too. Many men I know just want to be strong for their wives, but I wanted to know how he needed to care for himself too. **Turns out, what he needed was physical activity (he cut down several trees on our property, built things, fixed things) and needed to be outside a lot. He had to be active, always doing something.** *Once I understood he needed these things as much as I needed him to just listen to me talk through my emotions, I was much more forgiving of his time doing these things. At first, I thought he was just trying to stuff his grief, or wasn't grieving at all, but in reality those things were as therapeutic to him as blogging and connecting with other moms was to me. I wish he could have told me that sooner, but I am so glad we eventually did have that conversation and were able to help each other more and find a balance.*

Lacy -
One thing that helped us both early on was acknowledging that we were both processing our daughter's death in different ways. And that the communication/emotional differences that existed before her loss were still there...I learned to turn to other friends to help me process through some of those complicated things. He wanted to love me and support me, but understanding our different needs emotionally (like his need to sometimes keep the box of his emotions regarding Naomi's death closed) helped us remain together in the grief while still giving each other space.

Men and Women Grieve Differently

William -
I often wish I would have been able to express more openly to my wife the amount of grief I was having. I was too busy worrying about comforting her that I did not want to admit to myself how much I was affected.

Anthony -
Stephanie always wanted to talk about Oaken, even when she was pregnant, that hasn't changed... I don't feel like I have that

great of a bond, since all I did was stand back and watched the emotional rollercoaster she was on, I let her... I never really wanted to talk about him... I remember one day after an appointment, she was talking about Oaken and questioned me on why I never talk about him... My reply was **simple "Just because I don't talk about him, doesn't mean it doesn't hurt."**

Jacob -
With Sufficient Grace the doulas that helped out kept reminding us that that was the case, and we needed to be able to grieve differently.

Jamie -
Men suffer because their wives suffer so greatly. In the moment, they need to be strong, someone has to take care of the other children, go to work to provide for the family, etc. They don't have the time to grieve. In many ways, their grief expresses through service to their wife and family, with occasional surprises when they break down sobbing in the car thinking about what will now never be.

Ryan -
I felt like that as a man I could have benefitted from another man who had taken a similar journey reaching out to me in my grief process. Initially people would ask me how I was doing and of course I would tell them that I was okay. I felt like there wasn't anyone who understood so I would give this as a scripted response just to move the conversation along. I wanted to be okay and I wanted to be there to help my wife heal, to be there for her at any moment. I delayed the grieving process to ensure I was the "strong one". I wished someone would have told me that we needed to grieve more together as a couple instead of everyone wanting us to quickly get through this process. I needed another man to tell me that it wasn't up to me to carry this grief on my own back. I was running from grief as much as possible and it wasn't healthy. I embraced the grief process more after I knew my wife was on solid ground medically.

You can see where the lines of communication can get crossed, and misunderstandings can occur between husbands and wives in the midst of grief. Here are just a few words of wisdom we have gleaned:

1. Respect each other's need to grieve differently. If at all possible, do not do things that may bring pain to your spouse. At the same time, do not deprive yourself of doing the things you feel you need to do to honor your baby your way. Find a way to honor your baby that also honors the feelings of your spouse.

2. Find time to laugh and do things that you enjoy together. Grieving is hard, heavy work. Find some time to keep it light.

3. Keep life as simple as you can. Try not to take on too much for your family schedule. Protect yourselves and each other from extra stress or things that may bring unneeded sorrow.

4. Find ways to honor the memory of your baby as a family.

5. Communicate with love and respect.

6. Take comfort in physical affection. Do not turn away from each other, but turn toward each other.

7. Pray together and for each other. God is able to mend your broken hearts and keep your marriage. Guard your marriage and bathe it in prayer You may feel too weak to pray sometimes. That's okay. Saying, "God, help me...it hurts too much to even pray" is still a prayer. It's been a prayer of mine many times.

Two are better than one,
Because they have a good reward for their labor.
For if they fall, one will lift up his companion.
But woe to him who is alone when he falls,
For he has no one to help him up.
Again, if two lie down together,
they will keep warm;
But how can one be warm alone?
Though one may be overpowered by another,
two can withstand him.
And a threefold cord is not quickly broken.
~Ecclesiastes 4:8-12

What Was Helpful and Not-So-Helpful

Josh -
Not so helpful is how the fathers don't get included much even though we hurt too. Helpful is finding some online groups for dads to express our thoughts and feelings.

Brian -
The impactful thing that the hospital/funeral home/others can do, both positive and negative, is to remember us and our son. Some of the most joyful moments are when others independently remember William. Conversely, some of the most painful moments are when people forget about William; when the nurse at the post-partum visits assumes your son is alive while she has your file in her hand that states otherwise. We will never forget William and the life he had.

Matt -
Our hospital was great. They had 2 nurses who were in charge of parents/instances of stillborn, and they guided us wonderfully. They recommended things to do, what needed to be done at the time, and what could wait. They reached out to us after we left the hospital, checking in with how we were doing. They sent out reminders of child loss groups that met at the hospital. Something that was hard for us is how little other people understood what happened. And you can't really understand what happened unless you have been through it, so I don't expect people to understand us and what we are feeling. But in the world of technology we live in, I expected people to do some research about the topic. There are blogs upon blogs about this topic, and there are a lot of good resources on things you should/shouldn't do, things to say/not to say. The biggest help I can give people who have not been through this is research. Try to have an understanding of what we are going/went through.

William -
Communication about the experience has been helpful. Making sure as a husband to let my wife know that although I may not fully understand her feelings I will always be there to listen and comfort her through anything she needs me to.

Anthony -
I know the doctor we switched to was amazing in Stephanie's eyes. To me she was just another doctor, who will get to poke at our baby. We didn't know the gender of our baby till about 4wks before he was here, and with the old OB we tried to fight with him on why we wanted a blood test, to find out gender to plan for the funeral, he refused. I think that's the whole reason why she switched doctors, because she wasn't getting what she wanted with him... I would have done the same thing...
There isn't a lot of books for the dads, so more of those would be nice to see...
I guess just stuff to show that the fathers matter too.

Justin -
My wife and I could not grieve more differently. Hospitals are designed to push you out the door. They don't view your loss the same way that you do. Our funeral provider was fantastic and showed great care and concern for us. Find the people who want to help and want to understand. They are out there.

Jamie -
When our female doctor paused from caring for my wife, looked me straight in the eyes and asked specifically how I was handling the sadness and grief and then listened to the answer.

Ryan -
Our son was delivered early to save the life of my wife. After he was birthed, he was wrapped in a blanket and put on a cart and everyone walked away from him to tend to my wife. I had to speak up and ask if I could hold him. I needed to hold him. Of course they said yes. While I didn't realize the criticalness of the situation, they were putting all of their efforts into trying to save my wife from dying, and she was their number one priority that

day. *This really stung and continues to sting. My son was dead, but there was no moment where the doctor or nurse presented him to us and asked if I wanted to hold him. Everything else as far as care and empathy were amazing!*

Brian -
The biggest surprise that I had was the lack of printed resources for fathers. Luckily, I found a book by Emily Long, From Father to Father: Letters from Loss Dad to Loss Dad early in my grief and it helped immensely, to know that I was not alone. My wife and I did go to couple's therapy and to ParentShare at the local hospice center, Hosparus Health Grief Center. Through these interactions we learned to give space to each other and that we will process our feelings differently. Meeting other fathers is a great comfort; having a phone number to reach out on my terms is reassuring.

How Can Hospitals and Funeral Homes Best Support Bereaved Fathers

Ryan -

I feel like that through our experience hospitals really need to ensure there is some sort of way of collecting memories. The photos, handprints, certificate, and tangible items that were given to us mean the world to us as proof that he lived. As a father I was presented a baseball with our son's handprints. It sits in a glass case on a special shelf that we have reserved to the memory of our son. This ball means so much to me. We chose not to have a public memorial service. The funeral home was very respectful of our wishes. We had small items that we requested to be put in our son's hands. They also did not charge us for anything but the tiny casket which was an unexpected kindness.

Jacob -

The hospital can support us by letting us help. The nurse that we had was amazing. She had me bathe him and change his diaper. She even helped out with the pictures and anything else we needed. She was quite literally an angel to us. As for the funeral home, they helped out by walking me through the process (as my wife had more important things to worry about) and by providing the items at cost to us. The fact that it was very easy to take care of allowed me to support my wife better.

Brian -

The best thing that a hospital can do is allow a father to advocate for his family without bureaucratic barriers. When our son was born I did not feel excluded or denied information because I was not the mom/patient. This allowed me to expend what energy I had to caring for my family and not fighting organization regulations. Furthermore, the hospital respected my voice as if I was the patient and this allowed for a less painful experience for me. In closing, the best thing that any agency or entity can do for a father is to treat them as an equal to the mother; we both hurt.

Matt -
At the moment of losing your child, there's not much anyone can do to help. It's something that the husband and wife/mother and father have to figure out. Hospitals focus a lot on the mom, which is understandable because she is going through a lot of changes in her body and medically. But the only request I would have made is to have someone at the hospital or that the hospital could contact so that the father had someone to talk to. Preferably a dad who has been through this.

William -
Our hospital assigned a single nurse to us and I thought that was great...didn't have a bunch of different people in and out.

Anthony -
I feel I got lucky in this part. My dad works at the funeral home, so everything was covered. My dad even let me carry my son after Stephanie dressed him for the last time, to the crematorium. I cannot say much on this, funerals are something I try to avoid.... But if I had to give an answer... Just show empathy towards the father who just lost their baby.

Justin -
Give him decisions to make. The most difficult part in the early stages for me was just sitting and waiting. A man needs tasks to complete. He needs to have a purpose.

Josh -
Offer more support for the father's such as counseling and aftercare.

Zack -
Referrals to support groups and knowing what to expect as a father who has suffered through a miscarriage would be the most helpful.

Jamie -
By involving him in the conversation. It is his wife who carries the baby, but his lost dreams are just as real. Spending time asking how he is doing (not just her), or even (if he can talk/share) asking what specific future dreams (playing catch with his son, teaching his son to fish, etc.) he is having to say goodbye to.

Resources Fathers Wish Were Available To Them

As a Comfort Doula, I have provided support and resources for many mothers and fathers for many years. Providing adequate support and resources specifically for fathers has been an ongoing dilemma. Generally, support groups are more well-attended by women, often with little involvement from fathers. Because men and women grieve so differently, it can be a challenge to provide group support that involves mothers and fathers.

From reading some of the responses from the fathers interviewed and those we have worked with over the years, it seems it may be beneficial for fathers to have a place to go to just for the dads. This would allow for fathers to encourage one another in their own safe space, in their own language. Dads may also feel safer sharing their thoughts and struggles separate from their partners, because they may feel protective of the mother. They may be concerned about causing further pain to their partner. Many dads express the need to feel strong and supportive, which may hinder them from sharing their hurts in front of the mother.

Fathers often feel more comfortable "doing something" rather than just coming together for the sake of talking through their feelings. Planning an activity in a safe environment for grieving dads may result in a comfortable atmosphere where the men will share and process as they are in the midst of the "doing." Some dads may feel intimidated by the typical circle setting used in traditional support groups. Planning a golf outing, bowling, yard work, basketball game, building a memorial project, etc. may be a good way to connect grieving fathers and break the ice.

Men often express feelings with physical language. Recently two teenage brothers, scholar athletes; loved by our entire community and throughout the region, were tragically killed in a car accident. My son was best friends with one of the boys who died on that terrible day. Their close-knit group of friends has struggled through agonizing grief in the aftermath of their great loss. As a mother, I often learn the most sacred lessons about men from my sons. In their grief, they planned and hosted a candlelight vigil where they shared memories about their friends. Then they painted the parking space of one of the boys with his football number. They painted memorials at their favorite spot for pick-up basketball in twenty-degree weather. In their moments of anger, I thought it may be beneficial to physically break something, throw something, punch something. (Nothing that would cause them harm, of course!) I've watched them push themselves further athletically, pouring their emotions out on the field and on the track. They needed to get it out physically...every emotion.

Josh -
An actual father's group that meets in-person and more support and materials to fathers so they know that they are not alone.

Zack -
Support groups for fathers and resource lists for counselors that specialize in grief

Jacob -
Maybe a Facebook Group as going to meetings might be difficult and also resources that a father can use to make the process less stressful (list of funeral homes, cemeteries, and the process).

Brian -
I think more books are needed, and it would serve multiple functions. First, it would give fathers the words of other fathers; it would begin to break down the feelings of loneliness in our grief. Additionally, it would be something that someone can give to the bereaved father as a way of communicating when there are not the words for the emotions we feel. Furthermore, the reading may allow mother and father to participate in something together; my wife went to print resources in difficult times and it would be helpful for fathers to have something to turn to.

Matt -
Having a place for fathers to ask questions, and for fathers who have experienced this be able to answer them. Having some kind of digital group where you could post questions or just comments about what you are going through. Recommend things, advice against things, etc.

Anthony -
Books, social groups, I know there is a bunch on Facebook, because Stephanie is in a lot of them.

Justin -
I have often wondered this myself and have come up with nothing. There are many resources for mothers and couples. I read a lot of CS Lewis and the Bible. Anything that helps one to make sense of such unexpected and tragic death.

Jamie -
Some sort of framework/workbook/future memory book (maybe pick 2-3 childhood years, adolescent years, adult years) and make a place for a dad to identify with the source of his grief, i.e., what dreams he is saying goodbye to that are the hardest.

Ryan -
I feel like I would have attended a men's group if invited. I also feel like I would have benefitted from at least a couple of phone

calls. Maybe another loss dad just calling, or meeting for coffee. Men are sometimes the only ones that understand men.

Wrestling With Faith

It is normal for families to question God and faith during times of loss, tragedy, and grief. Some people may grow closer to God, while others may drift further away. Families need to know their feelings are valid and that every emotion is acceptable. It is okay to be angry with God, or to be confused about faith. He can handle it.

Susie -

After the devastation of the stillbirth last year, I found that I would pray probably 75 to 100 times each day for the twins, for over 5 months, waking in the night to pray as well. I don't understand why all the suffering, all the heartache, but I try to trust in the Lord and I try to be positive and think of when I will see them in heaven. It does not help much. I wanted to have them with their families here on earth. And then I feel guilty because God did not answer my prayers and I resent Him for that. And I dislike that a "friend" said to me, as the twins were fighting for life "the prayers of a righteous man availeth much." Bah, humbug, to that friend. That makes me either not righteous or not a man (person).

When You Can't Pray

From The Sufficient Grace Blog (Kelly Gerken)

I am strong. I have to be strong. Women of faith don't fall apart. Because God is big. And, we must not have much faith, if we fall apart.

I remembered that lie, from years before I sat beside my mother's bed at the hospice center, whispered by the slithering one as I ran to the church restroom to hide the tears just weeks after I stood beside the tiny grave with the pink lined casket, the one holding my only daughters. Christians don't grieve without hope. My babies were in heaven. Didn't I believe enough? Why was this smothering grief knocking me over? *I am strong. I have to be strong. People of faith don't fall apart.*

It was the same accusing lie when we heard the words incompatible with life in reference to our son, Thomas. *Where is your God now?* The voice questions, snarling. Stealing. Diminishing. Breaking. Twisting every truth I clung to desperately.

Don't you have enough faith? What lesson didn't you learn the first time, that another child has to die? Why are you wrestling to find the answers...don't good Christians blindly trust and accept...don't those who are truly faithful never wrestle with doubt or fear? Don't they know all the answers?

I didn't even try to answer that time. I just wept over my bible.

The months I carried Thomas sucker punched my faith more, blow after blow. I just kept reading. And, I learned that being faithful doesn't mean not feeling doubt or fear. Faith is trusting God anyway...when you're most afraid and filled with doubt and questions. Believing when you don't see.

Those weeks in the hospice center, I sang to her. I read the Word to her. I prayed over her. I answered the questions of those around me. I was strong. Except for the day my baby brother had to carry me out, because I temporarily lost my mind to grief and exhaustion. Otherwise, I was strong. I had to be strong. That's what women of faith do, right?

I was a woman of faith. My God is big. Only, underneath, I was really more like the girl who had to be carried out by her baby brother as she fell to pieces in front of his eyes.

After my mother died, when He finally took her home, I couldn't pray. For the first time in my life, I couldn't talk to the God who carried me.

I told my pastor, "I can't pray right now. It's really bothering me. Every time I try to pray, I can't...all I can say is: 'I'm sorry God, I can't talk to you right now. It just hurts too much.'"

My pastor said, "That's still prayer."

I have thought of that truth often. And, many times, when grief is raw and you feel stripped naked, beaten to the core with the pain and disappointment of it all....how. How could our God, our big loving Father God...let this happen? Why didn't He listen to our prayer? Was it because we aren't worthy...aren't enough...didn't pray right...didn't have enough faith? Why?

Grieving hearts ask those hard questions. I don't have all the answers; although, God has been patient to teach me many things in the surrendering and trusting, over the years. But, the longer I walk this journey, and the more brokenness I see along the way, I'm convinced that for some things, there are no answers this side of heaven. I can say all the words...and they're even true...those words...that God is good, that nothing separates us from His love, that He will never leave us nor forsake us...even in the darkest pits of despair. I can say them and I can promise that I've seen Him keep those promises in my own life. But, it won't take away the pain a heart feels when that which is most sacred has been ripped from her, and her heart lays in pieces at her feet.

Yes...it is a freeing, healing, soul-balming surrender to offer broken praise to heaven...and the sound is sweet to God's ears. He loves the broken praise. And, somehow showers healing back to us in the midst of the offering. But, if you can't muster it through the pain just yet....if it hurts beyond words forming on lips. If you are just too hurt to talk to him right now, tell Him that much. Yell, scream, cry, sit there in silence.

That's still prayer.

He hears you, even when you can't utter the words. He hears the words of your broken heart, catches the falling tears in a bottle, and thinks of you more than the grains of sand on the longest beach. Even if you can't bear to talk to Him right now. Even if nothing He has allowed makes one ounce of human sense to your betrayed, broken heart. Even then, He holds you. He loves you. And, He fights for you.

And, that's still prayer.

The truth is, I am weak. My faith is small. But, my God, He is strong. And, my God is big. Big enough for my broken. And, big enough for your broken, too.

And I am convinced that nothing can ever separate us from God's love. Neither death nor life, neither angels nor demons, neither our fears for today nor our worries about tomorrow—not even the powers of hell can separate us from God's love. No power in the sky above or in the earth below—indeed, nothing in all creation will ever be able to separate us from the love of God that is revealed in Christ Jesus our Lord. – Romans 8:38-39

From One Father to Another

Kyle talks about perspective -
Something that really helped me was this revelation: **Don't focus so far ahead. I only needed to make it through the next minute, then the next... God would be in every single minute.**

When Josiah was born, we had no idea that he would be born with a diaphragmatic hernia. Nothing had been diagnosed in the womb. The hospital crew took him from Lynnette very quickly and left. Lynnette said, "Follow them!", so I did. They stabilized Josiah, the doctor told me that things weren't looking good and might die.

I left NICU in shock! I couldn't believe that after already losing a baby (Samuel), we'd have to endure loss yet again. Walking back to Lynnette's room, the thought occurred to me, "I'm going to have to tell my wife that our new son might die". My heart hurt beyond description. I was walking back to tell her what was happening and the tears were beginning to fall. I ran into the bathroom, locked the door fell on my face and sobbed, crying to God, "Please spare us this! Not again! Lord, Help me! I need your peace, please God please!" In that moment, I experienced a miracle, God's peace flooded over me and I became calm.

Over the next 5 days, as we visited our son in NICU, I prayed over him, read the bible to him, wrote in my journal, and sang praises to God. It wasn't the same man that entered that bathroom!

The point to all this is to encourage fathers to run to the Heavenly Father first and beg for His peace. When we desire to be strong for our families, he will give us the courage, strength and peace to endure. still marvel when I think back to that time in the hospital. Those 5 days changed my perspective forever.

Stacy -
Discussing it with fathers who have had the same tragedy in their lives is helpful. Father's carry added guilt and pressure as the protector of the family unit so it would be good to relate to other fathers. I still carry shame and guilt for my lack of urgent action the night my daughter grew ill. Of course I know it was out of my hands but still – reflecting back it is hard to let those specifics go. It can also be really hard to enjoy the things that you used to before the tragedy. Keeping hobbies, listening to music, and continue to find good things in life despite the terrible pain is very hard for men to do.

Aaron -
For me, it would have been pastoral or chaplain support, as I mentioned above, but also, it would have meant so much to me just to know that there was an organization or counseling agency that specialized in situations like ours that I could turn to if I wanted to seek help.

At those moments when I considered getting professional help, I didn't know where to turn because I didn't feel that a standard community mental health organization or a general counselor/therapist was the answer. roller-coaster of emotions that I dealt with in our situation, I felt, could have only been understood by someone who specialized in these types of cases. This is insight solely from my perspective.

Mark -
I think having some literature written from the men's perspective would be really nice (This is a great idea, and I love that you're doing this!!!). A phone call a few weeks later from a father who has been through something like this, would also be helpful, unless it was clear the father didn't want anything like that.

Tim -
Keep going to church, spend time doing things you enjoy, and be there for your wife.

Zack -

The pain from losing a child can feel overwhelming at times. It's hard wanting to make everything better, trying to protect my wife from the pain and shield my family from suffering, leaving me feeling more alone than ever at times. I would tell any newly bereaved father to not forget to take care of themselves and that it's okay to cry over the loss of your baby.

Jacob -

To put it bluntly you will be forgotten. When you tell people what has happened the first thing people say is "how is your wife doing?". It will sting a little. Try and remember that you are a father and that you had a little one. That is something that cannot be forgotten.

As a newly bereaved dad know that you are not alone. Unfortunately, you have joined a fraternity of men that have gone though one of the most horrible things imaginable. Do not close yourself off to your family. Be vulnerable to your wife, but show her that you are strong and lead your family to a place of healing, whatever and wherever that may be. Be open and honest. The cliché saying is true, it does get better.

Scott -

Be there for your wife. Even if you have a crappy day at work, your wife may have had an even worse one dealing with the grief of losing your child.

Brian -

You are not alone. You can survive this. What you are going through will change you forever. Ask for help.

When I talked to my wife about getting professional help for myself, I was at least a week behind what she had seen coming. While I worked in a field that required me to be aware of the symptoms of depression, anxiety, and addiction, and even I was slow to seek guidance.

When I accepted that change was going to be daily routine things got better. In my experience, I have become more self-aware of my emotions, attitude, and demeanor. This awareness has allowed me to choose who I want to be for my wife, my son, and myself. Some days are better than others, but they all help me learn about how I am evolving as a person.

Matt -
My biggest advice is to talk about it. Keeping it bottled up will lead to nothing good. It's okay to grieve, it's okay to show these feelings. Too much we are told that men need to be manly, that we can't show feelings, we have to be tough. Being tough doesn't help you get through this. Losing your child will tear any man down, and it will destroy their world for a moment. You need to share, hopefully with the mother of the child. If not with them, with someone who has gone through this. People who haven't experienced child loss don't understand. And they can't.

William -
Make sure you stay in contact with your spouse...she is going to go through a variety of emotional and mental states and she needs you to be her rock. Don't be pushy with her but instead remind her that when she needs you, you are there to give her whatever support she may need.

Anthony -
Don't lose hope, don't be quick to give up. As long as your baby has a heartbeat, your baby is alive... Talk to your baby, if you don't want your wife/girlfriend to see you talking to your baby, do it while she sleeps... When you see your baby, nothing else matters in the world, your baby is perfect... Let your girl talk about your baby, we walk this path together but our views of the horizon are different. Cherish the moments you do have.

Justin -
Support your wife. Give her all you have. If you are fortunate enough to have other children prior to your loss, invest your energy in them. Your role as the leader of your family will never be more tested than at this time. You will fail, you will fall; but you have to get back up. They are counting on you, looking to you.

46

Jamie -

I know your pain, and I want you to know that your grief and loss is real, even if you did not carry the baby in your belly. You dreamed of their future in your heart. And that is enough. Write down those dreams as you say goodbye to them, so that someday, you can share them with your spouse and cry together.

Ryan -

What would I say to a newly bereaved dad? I am sorry that you have had this experience. Your life as you know it will be different now. The world continues to turn, sometimes faster than you are ready to go. Life is not over, just different. Your child's life mattered and forever will matter. Speak their name often, let others know that it is okay to talk about it with you. (If that is okay with you). God loves you and will bring you through everything. There is nothing wrong with taking time to grieve. Retreat to the arms of your God and your wife. Take time to pray and ask for strength. Strap on the armor of God and face the world with courage. Your child wants you to be happy! The world is a tough place and it will eat you up if you don't deal with your feelings. Find a trusted buddy that you can lean on in addition to your spouse. As men we always tell others "If you need anything at all, let me know." Be open to receiving the help offered to us. Don't let anyone tell you to "get over it".

Jeff -

Honest, Humble Reflections from a Dad

Back at the time of our two miscarriages, I could have been described as completely cold and unsupportive. I did what I knew how to do well: work. I didn't understand the pain my wife was going through. Sadly, I didn't try to understand. I can't rewrite history. But I can allow others to teach me in the present. A recent grad school project has given me the incredible opportunity to hear others' stories, and to gain a much needed, new perspective. From this process, I know for certain that we dads may be shy about our feelings, and we may avoid the idea of a support group, but we really need each other. Grieving is different for us, but a group context, even if we just meet to watch a basketball game or eat or both, could connect us in a healing way.

Jeff (continued) -
The poem I wrote, (honoring my wife's sacred work) in the process
of working with couples who have experienced loss:
"Blessed ... to have friends like you,
Honored ... to hear your story anew.
God is so gracious, I ask "Why me?"
Thankful for my angel named T,
who so naturally,
with humility,
offers empathy.
She makes a close friend,
while I sometimes offend.
I have so much to learn,
as for crying, it's my turn,
While I am driving away;
God's peace be with you I pray!

One beautiful father summed up the heart of what a parent faces when saying goodbye to his child, while trying to comfort and encourage his grief-stricken wife.

She said, "If I hold her, it means she is gone."

And, he said, "No, it means she was here."

She was here. Our babies were here. And, everything we do...every breath we take...every step...every moment is touched by the truth that our babies, for however brief a time, were here. They lived.

Greg Laurie (famous pastor and bereaved father) –
Some people seem to expect us to "recover" at some point. As someone who lost three family members in a car crash wrote, "We recover from broken limbs, not amputations. Catastrophic loss, by definition, precludes recovery. It will transform us or destroy us, but it will never leave us the same. There is no going back to the past, which is gone forever; only going ahead to the future, which is yet to be discovered."

I will never "recover" or "go back to normal," because that would imply going back to life the way it was before. Life will not be the same without my son.

So now, I am living a new kind of normal.
(interview with Huffington Post)

Grief and Remembering

There are stages of grief that most people go through: denial, anger, bargaining, depression, acceptance. Others describe numbness, disorganization, and reorganization. Each individual is unique in their grief. A variety of responses are "normal" and can be expected, such as: anger, resentment, pain, sorrow, bitterness, emptiness, numbness, exhaustion, apathy, depression, and even some joy as you remember your loved one, peace as you think of your loved one in heaven. There are so many feelings that come at will and even when the overwhelming sorrow has passed and a new form of "normalcy" has returned, you may out of nowhere, when you least expect it, feel grief's gripping waves overtake you once more.

You may not feel the same things at the same time as your partner. You may not need as many outward, tangible memories as your wife. There are still special ways you can honor the memory of your baby together.

Taking the time to remember a loved one is an important and precious part of the grieving process. Some find comfort in journaling, creating a memory book of pictures and memories of the moments that make up our lives together. Sometimes it's the simple everyday memories that mean the most- a smile, a touch, a hug, a laugh, a smell. In the case of losing a baby or a child whose life was cut short, we not only feel the empty loss of the person, but also of all the dreams we hold for that precious life that ended so suddenly.

Attend a memorial ceremony together, light a candle, plant a tree or garden, donate to a favorite charity, include your baby's memory in traditions (Christmas ornaments, etc.), celebrate birthdays, build something special.

You should choose to honor your baby's memory in ways that mean something to you. It doesn't have to fit in a mold that others set. It should mean something special to you and your family.

Some fathers pour themselves into their work or delve into a new hobby. It may be helpful to find healthy outlets for your feelings, especially if you're not comfortable expressing emotions.

Keep talking to your partner. And, don't be afraid to remember. There's nothing wrong with a few tears falling. Hers or yours.

Your baby is worth remembering. And, your grief is worth feeling.

Steven Curtis Chapman
(famous musician speaking of the loss
of his five-year old daughter):

"We have talked a lot. And you will hear all of us talk
about
the process of grieving with hope.
That's what has kept us breathing, kept us alive,
is that while we are grieving this process,
there is a hope that we have that we're anchored to
in the midst of just what sometimes seems unbearable."

(2009 Good Morning America interview on ABC)

It must be very difficult
To be a man in grief,
Since "men don't cry"
and "men are strong"
No tears can bring relief.

It must be very difficult
To stand up to the test,
And field the calls and visitors
So she can get some rest.

They always ask if she's all right
And what she's going through.
But seldom take his hand and ask,
"My friend, but how are you?"

He hears her crying in the night
And thinks his heart will break.
He dries her tears and comforts her,
But "stays strong" for her sake.

It must be very difficult
To start each day anew.
And try to be so very brave-
He lost his baby too.

Eileen Knight Hagemeister

Helpful Resources

Online
(for families facing a fatal diagnosis and/or for those experiencing loss)

sufficientgraceministries.org
perinatalhospice.org
stillstandingmag.com
nowilaymedowntosleep.org
benotafraid.net
stringofpearlsonline.org
fathersgrievinginfantloss.blogspot.com

Books

Walking With You for Grieving Fathers
Empty Arms
A Gift of Time (for families facing a life limiting or fatal diagnosis in pregnancy)
I'll Hold you in Heaven
I Will Carry You
Between Heaven & the Real World – Steven Curtis Chapman
Heaven is for Real
Dreams of You Memory Book
Walking With You Booklet
A Guide for Fathers ~ When a Baby Dies (Tim Nelson)

For Siblings

The Story of Hope – Helping Kids Express Feelings of Grief and Loss
Heaven is for Real for Kids
Someday Heaven
Someday we'll play in Heaven
Sibling Grief Wintergreen Press

Made in the USA
Columbia, SC
25 June 2021